Writing Yellow Pages

for Students and Teachers

from The KIDS' STUFF™ People

Incentive Publications, Inc.
Nashville, TN

Special acknowledgement is accorded to

- *The KIDS' STUFF™ People for compiling
  and organizing the materials included
  in this publication*
- *Susan Eaddy for the cover design*
- *Sally Sharpe, Editor*

ISBN 0-86530-038-0
Library of Congress Catalog Card Number 87-83366

Table of Contents

IDEAS FOR EXPANDING A WRITING VOCABULARY

- Look for new words in every book you read. Practice pronouncing and writing them.

- Learn to spell one new word every day.

- Read catalog descriptions to find words used to influence consumers to buy catalog items. Use the words in some written form within three days.

- Pick a word.
  - ___ Write rhyming words.
  - ___ Use it to make new words.
  - ___ List synonyms.
  - ___ List antonyms.
  - ___ List homonyms.
  - ___ List heteronyms.
  - ___ Write a paragraph about the word.
  - ___ Look up the meaning in your dictionary.
  - ___ Write it like it feels.
  - ___ Use it as the basis for a collage.
  - ___ Challenge a friend to spell it.

- Write a play you'd like for your class to present. Be sure to make the dialogue interesting, entertaining, and original.

- Play Scrabble, Word Bingo, Spell-O, and Boggle.

- Make regular deposits in your own word and phrase bank. Use these as starters, and add more of your own.

  Linking Words:

however	moreover	therefore	furthermore
hence	meanwhile	whereas	nevertheless

  Words That Show Time Order:

later	before	finally	earlier
first	then	next	afterward

- Make lists of words and phrases that:
  - ___ Add pizazz
  - ___ Create excitement
  - ___ Describe
  - ___ Arouse curiosity
  - ___ Demand attention
  - ___ Build suspense

- Write to a pen pal, preferably one your own age who lives in another country. Use interesting and descriptive words and phrases to tell about yourself, your home, and your own particular interests.

7

- Use a guide to free and inexpensive learning materials to find three sets of information materials you would like to have. Select materials on topics you know little or nothing about, and write letters requesting the materials.

- Keep a diary—make it personal and private.

- Become a list-maker. Start with lists of:
  ___ Things To do
  ___ Wishes
  ___ TV and radio programs
  ___ Names and addresses
  ___ Important events
  ___ Places to go
  ___ Things to see
  ___ Budgets

- Design your own greeting cards complete with original messages from you!

- Pick out and pronounce the rhyming words as you read poetry.

- Read cookbooks, game books, and other books giving directions in a sequential manner. Make a list of the words used frequently to tell the reader "what to do," "when to do," and "how to do."

- Make a list of twenty careers that interest you. Use your dictionary or thesaurus to find one or more unusual synonyms for each of the careers.

- Write a letter to your senator or representative about a matter of concern to you. Use ten words that you've never used before in a letter.

- Look in the Yellow Pages of the telephone book to find words frequently used in ads. Just for fun, make a list of all the three-syllable words that are used more than three times on one page.

- Daydream, and then write your dreams.

- Make a list of your friends and family members and their birthdays. Send one of your original greeting cards to each one on the appropriate day.

- Hang a large piece of paper on a wall in your room. Each time you learn a new word, write the word in fancy script on the paper. Use lots of different colors to make your "word wall" interesting and attractive.

THINGS TO WRITE ON

stationery, tablets, pads, notebooks
acetate
file folders
fabric
index cards
tissues
grocery sacks, shopping bags
gift bags
paper towels
kites
* your hands and feet (or someone
    else's, with their permission)
*bodies
  gift-wrap paper
  canvas
  cardboard, poster board, tagboard
  construction paper
  tissue paper
  cakes
  cookies
  adding machine tape
  old window shade
  plastic tablecloth
  hats
  T-shirts
  old lamp shades
  paper plates and cups
  wooden spoons
  shirt boards
*bathtubs
*sinks
  leaves, stones, and rocks
*shovels
*mirrors
*windows
  toilet paper
  wood strips, shingles
*cookie sheets
*pot lids
*sidewalks, streets
  bricks and concrete blocks
*drinking glasses
*sunglasses
*dust pans
*plastic plates, cups, and glasses
*Formica table tops
*glass table tops
*refrigerator doors
  old wallpaper
  fingers of a glove
  boxes

THINGS TO WRITE WITH

pencil
pen
chalk
paint
soap
shoe polish
shaving cream
toothpaste
feather
lipstick
cake frosting
yarn or twine
glue
mud
twigs and sticks
paintbrushes
sponges
ribbon
string
tape
fingers and toes
shells
stones
syrup
pudding
salt
buttons
rope
beans
seeds
cereal
nails and tacks
rags and cotton balls
blocks
letters cut from magazines, newspapers,
    bulletins, and brochures
paper punched holes
needle and thread
embroidery thread
dental floss
words cut from greeting cards
paper clips (glued together
    or placed end to end)
string beans
spaghetti
pretzel sticks
whipped cream
crayons
wet ashes
felt markers
press-on letters

*Be sure to use water-soluble writing materials on these!

THINGS TO WRITE

ads
advice columns
allegories
anecdotes
announcements
anthems
apologies
autobiographies
awards

ballads
bedtime stories
billboards
biographies
blurbs
books
book jackets
book reviews
brochures
bulletins
bumper stickers

calendar quips
campaign speeches
captions
cartoons
catalog entries
cereal boxes
certificates
character sketches
church bulletins
cinquains
comic strips
commercials
comparisons
complaints
constitutions
contrasts
conundrums
conversations
couplets
critiques

crossword puzzles

definitions
descriptions
dialogues
diaries
diets
directions
directories
documents
dramas

editorials
encyclopedia entries
epilogues
epitaphs
essays
evaluations
exaggerations
exclamations
explanations

fables
fairy tales
fantasies
fashion show scripts
feature articles
folklore
free verse

gags
good news/bad news
gossip
graffiti
greeting cards
grocery lists

haiku
headlines
horoscopes
"how-to" booklets
hymns

indexes
inquiries
interviews
introductions
invitations

jingles
job applications
jokes
journals

legends
letters
limericks
lists
love notes
lyrics

malapropisms
marquee notices
memos
menus
metaphors
minutes
monologues
movie reviews
mysteries
myths

newscasts
newspapers
notes
novels
nursery rhymes

obituaries
observations
odes
opinions

palindromes
pamphlets

parodies
persuasive letters
phrases
plays
poems
post cards
prayers
predictions
product descriptions
proformas
profound sayings
prologues
propaganda
proposals
protest letters
proverbs
puns
puppet shows

questions
quips
quizzes
quotations

ransom notes
real estate notices
rebuttals
recipes
record covers
remedies
reports
requests
Requiems
resumés
reviews
rhymes
riddles

sales pitches
satires
sayings

science fiction
secrets
self-portraits
sentences
sequels
serialized stories
sermons
signs
slogans
songs
sonnets
speeches
spoofs
spook stories
spoonerisms
sports accounts
stories
summaries
superstitions

tall tales
telegrams
telephone directory
television scripts
textbooks
thank you notes
theater programs
titles
tongue twisters
travel brochures
tributes
trivia

vignettes
vitas

want ads
warnings
weather forecasts
wills
words

THINGS TO WRITE ABOUT

Things to Write About	Date	Comments
Adventure		
Art		
Bodies of Water		
Books		
Communication		
Current Events		
Daydreams		
Families		
Fantasies		
Feelings		
Folklore		
the Future		
Gardening and Farming		
Geography		
Ghosts, Goblins, Witches, Fairies, Elves, and Trolls		
History		
Hobbies		
Holidays		
Land Formations		
Long Ago		
Manners		
Money		
Music		
Politics		
Problems		
Propaganda		
Religion		
Scenery		
Science		
Seasons		
Social Events		
Someone Else's Life		
Sports		
a Town, City, or Country		
Tragedy		
Transportation		
Travel		
Trivia		
the Unknown		
the Weather		
Your Life		

WORD LISTS TO MAKE AND KEEP

Feeling words
Sound words
Color words
Time words
Friendly words
Unfriendly words
Number words
City words
Country words
Day words
Night words
Home words
School words
Art words
Theater words
Food words
Ocean words
Valley words
Hill words
Jungle words
Mountain words
Desert words
Seashore words
Shopping words
Appreciation words
Disappointment words
Sad words
Glad words
Clothing words
Fashion words
Suspense words
Fat words
Thin words

Holiday words
Hate words
Adventure words
Store words
Family words
Religious words
Taste words
Love words
Hot words
Cold words
Circus words
Goodbye words
Hello words
Airplane words
Train words
Truck words
Automobile words
Swimming words
Football words
Golf words
Space words
Advertising words
Tennis words
Baseball words
Basketball words
Scratchy words
Yes words
No words

Election words
Size words
Shape words
War words
Peace words
Nonsense words
Season words
Weather words
Radio words
Newspaper words
TV words
Career words
Baby words
Children's words
Teen-age words
Adult words
Teacher words
Pizazz words
Nature words
Music words
Feminine words
Masculine words
Library words
Tax words
Mineral words
Plant words
Animal words
Hotel words
Restaurant words
Health words
Gym words
Excitement words
Fear words

Start your own "Big Book of Word Lists," and see
how long it takes you to add 100 or more categories
with at least five words in each category!

SIX STEPS IN THE WRITING PROCESS

1. Romancing

    This step describes a specific activity, discussion, piece of literature, or situation that will get students excited about a writing form or an idea. (Be sure to spend plenty of time on this stage.) When kids don't want to write or can't think of anything to say, they usually haven't been "romanced" enough.

2. Collecting

    This step is also a "romantic" stage. Collecting is the most fun and most creative part of the writing process. Ask questions, give directions, and make suggestions which will start ideas flowing and will help writers gather phrases, words, and thoughts to use as "raw material." This step goes quickly, so collect plenty of ideas. (You don't have to use all of the ideas, but you may choose from the assortment.)

3. Writing

    This step involves the giving of precise instructions and questions which will direct writers as they choose, organize, and combine "raw materials" into a written piece.

4. Praising

    This is a crucial step in the "criticism" stage. This is the stage in which good writing techniques are reinforced. The positive "judging" of a written piece should not be omitted. Make comments, observations, and suggestions to help students see the strengths of their writing. In this stage you will teach your writers to search for examples of good writing skills and to compliment one another on them. For example:

    "The phrase 'slippery, slinky snake' made me feel that I was actually touching a snake!"

    "You chose wonderful 'wet' words for this rain poem such as slush, drizzle, slurp, and soggy."

    "The opening word 'Crash!' really grabbed my interest."

5. Polishing

During this step you will make suggestions and ask questions to get writers to reorganize, refine, and rewrite their pieces. Try to emphasize one or two specific editing skills during each lesson. You can also teach kids to ask questions and make suggestions that are helpful to other writers. For example:

"It seems these two sentences say the same thing."

"The word 'pretty' is used so often. Why not use 'lovely' instead?"

"I think this idea might fit better in the next paragraph."

"The ending doesn't seem to pull everything together. Could you rewrite it so that the reader is not left with questions?"

"I'd like to know more about the main character. Could you add one more sentence?"

6. Showing Off

You give purpose and dignity to a piece of writing when you provide a way for writers to share what they've written. Provide students with the opportunity to "show off" their writing in one or more ways.

Note:

Be sure to instruct students to check and correct grammar, spelling, and mechanics at the "polishing" stage.

Adapted from COMPLETE WRITING LESSONS FOR THE PRIMARY GRADES, © 1987 by Incentive Publications, Inc., Nashville, TN. Used by permission.

RHYMING WORDS

wish	dream	boy	girl	match	love	miss
dish	cream	ahoy	curl	batch	above	bliss
fish	gleam	coy	hurl	catch	dove	hiss
squish	seam	enjoy	pearl	hatch	glove	kiss
swish	steam	joy	swirl	latch	of	sis
	team	toy	twirl	patch	shove	this

cat	bunk	ball	weak	think	rain
bat	clunk	call	beak	blink	cane
fat	drunk	crawl	cheek	brink	gain
flat	dunk	fall	leak	clink	lain
hat	hunk	gall	meek	drink	main
mat	junk	hall	peak	link	pain
pat	punk	mall	peek	pink	plane
rat	stunk	stall	reek	rink	stain
sat	sunk	tall	seek	sink	train
slat	trunk	wall	week	wink	vain

and	bare	black	block	blue	date
band	bear	back	clock	clue	ate
brand	care	crack	cock	crew	bait
canned	dare	lack	dock	drew	fate
fanned	fare	pack	flock	few	gate
gland	hair	quack	knock	flew	hate
grand	pear	rack	lock	glue	late
hand	rare	sack	mock	knew	mate
land	stare	smack	rock	new	rate
sand	there	stack	sock	to	state
stand	wear	track	tock	true	wait

day	dear	eye	four	friend	gold
clay	deer	by	core	bend	bold
gay	fear	cry	door	blend	bowled
hay	hear	fry	floor	end	cold
lay	here	high	more	lend	fold
may	near	I	pour	mend	hold
play	peer	lie	roar	pretend	mold
ray	queer	pie	sore	rend	old
say	rear	sigh	store	send	rolled
tray	steer	tie	tore	spend	sold
way	year	why	wore	tend	told

book	burn	time	fist	five	six	ten
brook	churn	crime	grist	chive	fix	been
cook	earn	dime	hissed	dive	kicks	den
crook	fern	grime	kissed	drive	licks	hen
hook	learn	lime	list	hive	picks	men
look	stern	rhyme	mist	jive	sticks	pen
rook	turn	slime	twist	live	ticks	when
took	yearn				wicks	yen

dog	thought	star	tin	bowl	man
cog	bought	are	bin	coal	ban
flog	brought	bar	din	foal	can
fog	caught	car	fin	goal	fan
frog	fought	far	gin	hole	pan
hog	ought	jar	kin	mole	plan
jog	sought	mar	pin	pole	ran
log	taught	tar	sin	roll	tan
smog	taut	scar	win	soul	van

grade	green	map	night	nine	ring
ade	bean	cap	bite	dine	bring
blade	clean	clap	bright	fine	cling
fade	dean	flap	fight	line	ding
glade	glean	gap	kite	mine	fling
laid	keen	lap	light	pine	king
made	lean	nap	quite	sign	sing
maid	mean	slap	right	swine	sling
paid	queen	tap	sight	tine	sting
raid	seen	trap	tight	vine	swing
wade	teen	wrap	white	whine	wing

room	run	tale	three	tone	snow
bloom	bun	dale	be	bone	blow
boom	done	fail	flea	cone	crow
broom	fun	gale	glee	groan	flow
doom	gun	hale	key	known	go
gloom	none	jail	knee	lone	know
groom	one	male	me	moan	low
loom	pun	nail	see	phone	mow
room	sun	pale	tea	stone	no
tomb	ton	rail	tree	thrown	row
zoom	won	sale	we	zone	so

SYNONYMS FOR WORDS COMMONLY USED
IN STUDENTS' WRITINGS

Amazing - incredible, unbelievable, improbable, fabulous, wonderful, fantastic, astonishing, astounding, extraordinary

Anger - enrage, infuriate, arouse, nettle, exasperate, inflame, madden

Angry - mad, furious, enraged, excited, wrathful, indignant, exasperated, aroused, inflamed

Answer - reply, respond, retort, acknowledge

Ask - question, inquire of, seek information from, put a question to, demand, request, expect, inquire, query, interrogate, examine, quiz

Awful - dreadful, terrible, abominable, bad, poor, unpleasant

Bad - evil, immoral, wicked, corrupt, sinful, depraved, rotten, contaminated, spoiled, tainted, harmful, injurious, unfavorable, defective, inferior, imperfect, substandard, faulty, improper, inappropriate, unsuitable, disagreeable, unpleasant, cross, nasty, unfriendly, irascible, horrible, atrocious, outrageous, scandalous, infamous, wrong, noxious, sinister, putrid, snide, deplorable, dismal, gross, heinous, nefarious, base, obnoxious, detestable, despicable, contemptible, foul, rank, ghastly, execrable

Beautiful - pretty, lovely, handsome, attractive, gorgeous, dazzling, splendid, magnificent, comely, fair, ravishing, graceful, elegant, fine, exquisite, aesthetic, pleasing, shapely, delicate, stunning, glorious, heavenly, resplendent, radiant, glowing, blooming, sparkling

Begin - start, open, launch, initiate, commence, inaugurate, originate

Big - enormous, huge, immense, gigantic, vast, colossal, gargantuan, large, sizeable, grand, great, tall, substantial, mammoth, astronomical, ample, broad, expansive, spacious, stout, tremendous, titanic, mountainous

Brave - courageous, fearless, dauntless, intrepid, plucky, daring, heroic, valorous, audacious, bold, gallant, valiant, doughty, mettlesome

Break - fracture, rupture, shatter, smash, wreck, crash, demolish

Bright - shining, shiny, gleaming, brilliant, sparkling, shimmering, radiant, vivid, colorful, lustrous, luminous, incandescent, intelligent, brilliant, knowing, quick-witted, smart, intellectual

Calm - quiet, peaceful, still, tranquil, mild, serene, smooth, composed, collected, unruffled, level-headed, unexcited, detached, aloof

Come - approach, advance, arrive, reach

Cool - chilly, cold, frosty, wintry, icy, frigid

Crooked - bent, twisted, curved, hooked, zigzag

Cry - shout, yell, yowl, scream, roar, bellow, weep, wail, sob, bawl

Cut - gash, slash, nick, sever, slice, carve, cleave, slit, chop, crop, lop, reduce

Dangerous - perilous, hazardous, risky, uncertain, unsafe

Dark - shadowy, unlit, murky, gloomy, dim, dusky, shaded, sunless, black, dismal, sad

Decide - determine, settle, choose, resolve

Definite - certain, sure, positive, determined, clear, distinct, obvious

Delicious - savory, delectable, appetizing, luscious, scrumptious, palatable, delightful, enjoyable, toothsome, exquisite

Describe - portray, characterize, picture, narrate, relate, recount, represent, report

Destroy - ruin, demolish, raze, waste, kill, slay, end, extinguish

Difference - disagreement, inequality, contrast, dissimilarity, incompatibility

Do - execute, enact, carry out, finish, conclude, effect, accomplish, achieve, attain

Dull - boring, tiring, tiresome, uninteresting, slow, dumb, stupid, unimaginative, lifeless, dead, insensible, tedious, wearisome, listless, expressionless, plain, monotonous, humdrum, dreary

Eager - keen, fervent, enthusiastic, involved, interested, alive to

End - stop, finish, terminate, conclude, close, halt, cessation, discontinuance

Enjoy - appreciate, delight in, to be pleased with, indulge in, luxuriate in, bask in, relish, savor, like

Explain - elaborate, clarify, define, interpret, justify, account for

Fair - just, impartial, unbiased, objective, unprejudiced, honest

Fall - drop, descend, plunge, topple, tumble

False - fake, fraudulent, counterfeit, spurious, untrue, unfounded, erroneous, deceptive, groundless, fallacious

Famous - well-known, renowned, celebrated, famed, eminent, illustrious, distinguished, noted, notorious

Fast - quick, rapid, swift, speedy, fleet, hasty, snappy, mercurial, swiftly, rapidly, quickly, snappily, speedily, lickety-split, posthaste, hastily, expeditiously, like a flash

Fat - stout, corpulent, fleshy, beefy, paunchy, plump, full, rotund, tubby, pudgy, chubby, chunky, bulky, elephantine, obese

Fear - fright, dread, terror, alarm, dismay, anxiety, awe, horror, panic, apprehension

Fly - soar, hover, flit, wing, flee, waft, glide, coast, skim, sail, cruise

Funny - humorous, amusing, droll, comic, comical, laughable, silly

Get -acquire, obtain, secure, procure, gain, fetch, find, accumulate, win, earn, reap, catch, net, bag, derive, collect, gather, glean, pick up, accept, come by, regain, salvage

Go - recede, depart, fade, disappear, move, travel, proceed

Good - excellent, fine, superior, wonderful, marvelous, suited, suitable, proper, capable, generous, kindly, friendly, gracious, obliging, pleasant, agreeable, pleasurable, satisfactory, well-behaved, obedient, honorable, reliable, trustworthy, favorable, profitable, advantageous, righteous, expedient, helpful, valid, genuine, ample, salubrious, estimable, beneficial, splendid, great, noble, worthy, first-rate, top-notch, grand, superb, respectable

Great - noteworthy, worthy, distinguished, remarkable, grand, considerable, powerful, much, mighty

Gross - improper, rude, coarse, indecent, crude, vulgar, outrageous, extreme, grievous, shameful, uncouth, obscene, low

Happy - pleased, contented, satisfied, delighted, elated, joyful, cheerful, ecstatic, jubilant, gay, tickled, gratified, glad, blissful, overjoyed

Hate - despise, loathe, detest, abhor, disfavor, dislike, disapprove, abominate

Have - hold, possess, own, contain, acquire, gain, maintain, bear, beget, occupy, absorb, fill

Help - aid, assist, support, encourage, back, wait on, attend, serve, relieve, succor, benefit, befriend, abet

Hide - conceal, cover, mask, cloak, camouflage, screen, shroud, veil

Hurry - rush, run, speed, race, hasten, accelerate, bustle

Hurt - damage, harm, injure, wound, afflict, pain

Idea - thought, concept, conception, notion, understanding, opinion, plan, view, belief

Important - necessary, vital, critical, indispensable, valuable, essential, significant, primary, principal, considerable, famous, distinguished, notable, well-known

Interesting - fascinating, engaging, sharp, keen, bright, intelligent, animated, spirited, attractive, inviting, intriguing, provocative, thought-provoking, challenging, inspiring, involving, moving, titillating, tantalizing, exciting, entertaining, piquant, lively, racy, spicy, engrossing, absorbing, consuming, gripping, arresting, enthralling, spellbinding, curious, captivating, enchanting, bewitching, appealing

Keep - hold, retain, withhold, preserve, maintain, sustain, support

Kill - slay, execute, assassinate, murder, destroy, abolish

Lazy - indolent, slothful, idle, inactive, sluggish

Little - tiny, small, diminutive, shrimp, runt, miniature, puny, exiguous, dinky, cramped, limited, itty-bitty, microscopic, slight, petite, minute

Look - gaze, see, glance, watch, survey, study, seek, search for, peek, peep, glimpse, stare, contemplate, examine, gape, ogle, scrutinize, inspect, leer, behold, observe, view, witness, perceive, spy, sight, discover, notice, recognize, peer, eye, gawk, peruse, explore

Love - like, admire, esteem, fancy, care for, cherish, adore, treasure, worship, appreciate, savor

Make - create, originate, invent, beget, form, construct, design, fabricate, manufacture, produce, build, develop, do, effect, execute, compose, perform, accomplish, earn, gain, obtain, acquire, get

Mark - label, tag, price, ticket, impress, trace, imprint, stamp, brand, sign, note, heed, notice, designate

Mischievous - prankish, playful, naughty, roguish, waggish, impish, sportive

Moody - temperamental, changeable, short-tempered, glum, morose, sullen, mopish, irritable, testy, peevish, fretful, spiteful, sulky, touchy

Move - plod, go, creep, crawl, inch, poke, drag, toddle, shuffle, trot, dawdle, walk, traipse, mosey, jog, plug, trudge, lumber, lag, run, sprint, trip, bound, hotfoot, high-tail, streak, stride, tear, breeze, whisk, rush, dash, dart, bolt, scamper, scurry, skedaddle, scoot, scuttle, scramble, race, chase, hasten, hurry, gallop, lope, accelerate, stir, budge, travel, wander, roam, journey, trek, ride, slip, glide, slide, slither, coast, sail, saunter, hobble, amble, stagger, prance, straggle, meander, perambulate, waddle, wobble, promenade, lunge

Neat - clean, orderly, tidy, trim, dapper, natty, smart, elegant, organized, spruce, shipshape, well-kept

New - fresh, unique, original, unusual, modern, current, recent

Old - feeble, frail, ancient, aged, used, worn, dilapidated, ragged, faded, broken-down, former, old-fashioned, outmoded, passé, veteran, mature, venerable, primitive, traditional, archaic, conventional, customary, stale, musty, obsolete

Part - portion, share, piece, allotment, section, fraction, fragment

Place - space, area, spot, region, location, position, residence, dwelling, set, site, station, status, state

Plan - plot, scheme, design, draw, map, diagram, procedure, arrangement, intention, contrivance, method, way, blueprint

Popular - well-liked, approved, accepted, favorite, celebrated, common, current

Predicament - quandary, dilemma, pickle, problem, plight, scrape, jam

Put - place, set, attach, establish, assign, keep, save, set aside, effect, achieve, do, build

Quiet - silent, still, soundless, mute, tranquil, peaceful, calm, restful

Right - correct, accurate, factual, true, good, just, honest, upright, lawful, moral, proper, suitable, apt, legal, fair

Run - race, speed, hurry, hasten, sprint, dash, rush, escape, elope, flee

Say/Tell - inform, notify, advise, relate, recount, narrate, explain, reveal, disclose, divulge, declare, command, order, bid, enlighten, instruct, insist, teach, train, direct, issue, remark, converse, speak, affirm, utter, express, verbalize, voice, articulate, pronounce, deliver, convey, impart, assert, state, allege, mutter, mumble, whisper, sigh, exclaim, yell, sing, yelp, snarl, hiss, grunt, snort, roar, bellow, thunder, boom, scream, shriek, screech, squawk, whine, philosophize, stammer, stutter, lisp, drawl, jabber, announce, swear, vow

Scared - afraid, frightened, alarmed, terrified, panicked, fearful, unnerved, insecure, timid, shy, skittish, jumpy, disquieted, worried, vexed, troubled, disturbed, horrified, terrorized, shocked, petrified, timorous, shrinking, tremulous, stupefied, paralyzed, stunned, apprehensive

Show - display, exhibit, present, note, point to, indicate, explain, reveal, prove, demonstrate, expose

Slow - unhurried, gradual, leisurely, late, behind, tedious, slack

Stop - cease, halt, pause, discontinue, conclude, end, finish, quit

Story - tale, myth, legend, fable, yarn, account, narrative, chronicle, epic, anecdote, memoir

Strange - odd, peculiar, unusual, unfamiliar, uncommon, queer, weird, outlandish, curious, unique, exclusive, irregular

Take - hold, catch, seize, grasp, win, capture, acquire, pick, choose, select, remove, steal, lift, rob, engage, purchase, buy, retract, recall, occupy, consume

Tell - disclose, reveal, show, expose, uncover, relate, narrate, inform, advise, explain, divulge, declare, command, order, bid, recount, repeat

Think - judge, deem, assure, believe, consider, contemplate, reflect, meditate

Trouble - distress, anguish, anxiety, worry, wretchedness, pain, danger, peril, disaster, grief, misfortune, difficulty, concern, inconvenience, effort

True - accurate, right, proper, precise, exact, valid, genuine, real, actual, steady, loyal, dependable, sincere

Ugly - hideous, frightful, frightening, shocking, horrible, unpleasant, monstrous, repulsive, terrifying, gross, gruesome, grisly, ghastly, horrid, unsightly, plain, homely, unattractive

Unhappy - miserable, uncomfortable, wretched, heartbroken, unfortunate, downhearted, sorrowful, depressed, dejected, melancholy, glum, gloomy, dismal, discouraged, sad

Use - employ, utilize, exhaust, spend, expend, consume, exercise

Wrong - incorrect, inaccurate, mistaken, erroneous, improper, unsuitable

WORDS THAT CONFUSE

ability (power), **capacity** (condition)

accede (agree), **exceed** (surpass)

accept (receive), **except** (exclude)

adapt (adjust), **adopt** (accept)

advise (to give advice), **advice** (counsel or recommendation)

affect (to influence), **effect** (result)

all ready (completely prepared), **already** (previously)

allude (to refer to), **elude** (escape)

allusion (reference), **illusion** (false perception), **delusion** (false belief)

assure (to set a person's mind at ease), **insure** (guarantee life or property against harm), **ensure** (to secure from harm)

avenge (to achieve justice), **revenge** (retaliation)

averse (opposition on the subject's part), **adverse** (opposition against the subject's will)

avoid (shun), **prevent** (thwart), **avert** (turn away)

between (use when referring to two persons, places, or things), **among** (use when referring to more than two persons, places, or things)

capital (seat of government), **capitol** (building)

censor (one who prohibits offensive material), **censure** (to criticize)

cite (to bring forward as support or truth), **quote** (to repeat exactly)

clench (to grip something tightly, as hand or teeth), **clinch** (to fasten firmly together)

complement (something that completes), **compliment** (an expression of praise)

compromise (a settlement in which each side makes concession), **surrender** (to yield completely)

confidant (one to whom secrets are told), **confidante** (a female confidant), **confident** (assured of success)

constant (unchanging), **continual** (repeated regularly), **continuous** (action without interruption)

consul (a country's representative in a foreign country), **council** (a deliberative assembly), **councilor** (member of a deliberative body), **counsel** (to give advice), **counselor** (one who gives advice)

contagious (transmissible by contact), **infectious** (capable of causing infection)

credible (plausible), **creditable** (deserving commendation), **credulous** (gullible)

deny (contradict), **refute** (to give evidence to disprove something), **repudiate** (to reject the validity of)

doubtless (presumption of certainty), **undoubtedly** (definite certainty)

elegy (a mournful poem), **eulogy** (a speech honoring a deceased person)

element (a basic assumption), **factor** (something that contributes to a result)

elicit (to call forth), **illicit** (unlawful)

emigrate (a single move by persons, used with *from*), **immigrate** (a single move by persons, used with *to*), **migrate** seasonal movement)

eminent (prominent), **imminent** (soon to occur)

farther (literal distance), **further** (figurative distance)

fatal (causing death), **fateful** (affecting one's destiny)

feasible (capable of happening), **possible** (that can be)

fewer (refers to units capable of being individually counted), **less** (refers to collective quantities or to abstracts)

graceful (refers to movement), **gracious** (courteous)

impassable (impossible to traverse), **impassive** (devoid of emotion)

imply (to hint or suggest), **infer** (to draw conclusions based on facts)

incredible (unbelievable), **incredulous** (skeptical)

insignificant (trivial), **tiny** (small)

insinuate (to hint covertly), **intimate** (to imply subtly)

invoke (to call upon a higher power for assistance), **evoke** (to elicit)

judicial (pertaining to law), **judicious** (exhibiting sound judgement)

latter (the second of two things mentioned), **later** (subsequently)

lay (to put or place), **lie** (to recline)

likely (use when mere probability is involved), **apt** (use when a known tendency is involved)

mania (craze), **phobia** (fear)

may (use when strong sense of permission or possibility is involved), **might** (use when weak sense of permission or possibility is involved)

mutual (refers to intangibles of a personal nature between two parties), **reciprocal** (refers to a balanced relationship in which one action is made on account of or in return for another)

nauseated (to feel queasy), **nauseous** (causing queasiness)

oblige (to feel a debt of gratitude), **obligate** (under direct compulsion to follow a certain course)

official (authorized by a proper authority), **officious** (extremely eager to offer help or advice)

older (refers to persons and things), **elder** (refers only to persons)

on (used to indicate motion to a position), **onto** (very strongly conveys motion toward), **on to** (use when *on* is an adverb and *to* is a preposition)

oral (refers to the sense of "word of mouth"; cannot refer to written words), **verbal** (can refer to both written and spoken words)

partly (use when stress is placed on a part in contrast to the whole), **partially** (use when the whole is stressed, often indirectly)

people (refers to a large group of individuals considered collectively), **persons** (refers to a small, specific number), **public** (a group of people sharing a common interest)

persecute (to oppress or harass), **prosecute** (to initiate legal or criminal action against)

piteous (pathetic), **pitiable** (lamentable), **pitiful** (very inferior or insignificant)

practically (almost), **virtually** (to all intents)

precipitant (rash, impulsive), **precipitate** (to hurl downward), **precipitous** (extremely steep)

principal (chief), **principle** (basic law or truth)

quite (very), **quiet** (hushed)

rack (a framework; to be in great pain), **wrack** (destruction by violent means)

raise (to move upward; to build; to breed), **rear** (to bring up a child), **rise** (to ascend)

rare (refers to unusual value and quality of which there is a permanent small supply), **scarce** (refers to temporary infrequency)

ravage (to devastate or despoil), **ravish** (to take away by force; to rape)

recourse (an application to something for aid or support), **resource** (an available supply)

regretful (sorrowful), **regrettable** (something that elicits mental distress)

reluctant (unwilling), **reticent** (refers to a temperament or style that is characteristically silent or restrained)

repel (drive off; cause distaste or aversion), **repulse** (drive off; reject by means of discourtesy)

respectfully (showing honor and esteem), **respectively** (one at a time in order)

restive (resistance to control), **restless** (lacking repose)

seasonal (refers to what applies to or depends on a season), **seasonable** (refers to timeliness or appropriateness to a season)

sensual (used when referring to the gratification of physical senses), **sensuous** (usually refers to senses involved in aesthetic gratification)

sit (to rest the body on the buttocks with the torso upright; usually intransitive), **set** (to put or place something; usually transitive)

specific (explicitly set forth), **particular** (not general or universal)

stationary (immovable), **stationery** (matched writing paper and envelopes)

tasteful (exhibiting that which is proper or seemly in a social setting), **tasty** (having a pleasing flavor)

transient (refers to what literally stays for only a short time), **transitory** (short-lived, impermanent)

turbid (muddy, dense; in turmoil), **turgid** (swollen; grandiloquent)

DESCRIPTIVE WORDS

acrid
aggressive
appreciative
archaic
atrocious
avaricious
avid
beautiful
bibulous
bombastic
bountiful
brackish
brilliant
brusque
bubbly
candescent
cankerous
cathartic
charismatic
charming
clairvoyant
coarse
colorful
comely
compassionate
conducive
contentious
cretaceous
daft
dangerous
dauntless
decorative
delirious
despiteous

dexterous
domineering
dour
dowdy
dreary
dubious
eager
effervescent
efficacious
elaborate
electrifying
elegant
evocative
extravagant
exuberant
fabulous
fantastic
fascinating
feeble
felicitous
fervent
fluorescent
fulgent
futile
gaudy
generous
gentle
glib
glorious
gorgeous
grandiloquent
gregarious
gushing
handsome

harmonious
haughty
hazardous
hilarious
horrendous
hysterical
ignominious
illuminant
illustrious
immaculate
impetuous
incredulous
ingenious
intriguing
jaunty
jocular
jolly
jubilant
judicious
jussive
kaleidoscopic
kind
knavish
knowledgeable
kooky
laborious
lank
lazy
lecherous
leisurely
lethargic
liquescent
lovely
luminous

luteous
magical
magnanimous
magnificent
majestic
massive
monstrous
mordacious
mystical
natural
nauseous
necessitous
nefarious
negligent
noctilucent
nonchalant
notorious
nummular
nutty
obedient
obese
obnoxious
obstinant
obstruent
octennial
offensive
ordinary
outrageous
painful
palpable
peaceful
pensive
pestiferous

picturesque
pleasant
pretty
putrid
quaint
quartz
quaternary
queasy
quirky
radiant
raucous
redivious
remorseful
renitent
repugnant
respectful
rickety
rugose
sapient
satirical
scrawny
scrupulous
sentimental
sharp
sinuous
sluggish
spectacular
splendid
stormy
stupendous
sweltering
taciturn
taut

tempestuous
tenacious
terrific
tingly
torrid
tremulous
tyrannical
ultraviolet
uncommon
undulant
unique
unwieldy
valiant
venomous
verbose
vicarious
vivacious
volatile
voracious
vulnerable
weak
whacky
whimsical
wiggly
withdrawn
witty
wonderful
xeric
xyloid
yellow
youthful
yummy
zealous

MEANINGS OF PREFIXES AND SUFFIXES

PREFIXES

ante	before	antecede
anti	against	antiwar
bi	two, twice	biweekly
co	together, with	copilot
counter	against	counterattack
de	down, away	descend
dis	not	displease
ex	out	export
fore	in front	foreground
in	not	incorrect
ir	not	irregular
mid	middle	midway
mis	wrong	misread
non	not	nonstop
post	after	postdate
pre	before, in front	preview
re	again	rewrite
sub	under	subway
tele	far away	telephone
trans	across	transatlantic
un	not	unkind

SUFFIXES

ance	state of being	importance
ar	one who does something	liar
en	having nature of	golden
er	one who does something	baker
ery	place which	bakery
ful	full of	successful
fy	form into	beautify
hood	state or rank	statehood
ible	able to	visible
ic	like, pertaining to	dramatic
ion	act, process of	action
ish	having nature of	wolfish
ist	one who	artist
less	without	toothless
ly	in the manner of	lovely
ment	action or process	payment
ness	state of being	friendliness
or	one who does something	actor
ous	state or condition	famous
ship	office or skill	championship
tion	act, process of	education

SPELLING HELPS

The following spelling rules are generalizations and do not work all of the time. However, they are often true, and are valuable spelling aids.

1. Each syllable of a word must contain one sounded vowel (al li ga tor).

2. A vowel is more likely to be pronounced short than long.

3. A vowel at the end of a one-syllable word is usually long (be).

4. The final *e* in a one-syllable word is usually silent (lake).

5. When *i* precedes *gh*, it is usually long (bright).

6. *I* comes before *e* except after *c*, or when sounded like *a* as in *neighbor*, and *weigh* (chief, receive).

7. Usually, a doubled consonant or vowel has one sound (letter, boot).

8. When two vowels are together, the first one usually says its own name (team).

9. The *ch* sound is often spelled *tch* (catch).

10. The *j* sound is often spelled *dg* or *dge* (dredging, smudge).

11. The *k* sound may be made by *c* or *ck* (came, stack).

12. The *gh* combination is usually silent (dough, fright), but sometimes it sounds like *f* (trough, laugh).

13. The consonants *c* and *g* are soft before *i*, *e*, and *y*; otherwise, they are hard (go, gentle; center, car).

14. The ending *-ance* may also be spelled *-ence* (endurance, presence).

15. The ending *-ous* may follow an *e* or an *i* (extraneous, delicious).

16. The ending *-tion* may be spelled *-cian, -sian, -sion,* or *-tian* (station, physician, Prussian, decision, Dalmatian).

17. Pluralize a word that ends with a *y* preceded by a consonant by changing the *y* to *i* and adding *es* (cry, cries).

18. The common prefixes *en-*, *in-*, and *un-* are not used interchangeably.

RULES FOR CAPITALIZATION

Capitalize the first letter in:

1. The first word of a sentence.

2. The first word in each line of poetry.

3. The first and all other important words in the greeting of a letter.

4. The first word in the closing of a letter.

5. The first, last, and other main words in titles of chapters, stories, poems, reports, songs, books, movies, and radio and television programs.

6. The word I.

7. A proper adjective.

8. Initials.

9. Titles of persons (Mr., Ms., Mrs., Dr.).

10. Abbreviations (P.O., R.R., C.O.D., Dr.).

11. Titles of high government officials.

12. A proper noun.

13. Words like mother, sister, and uncle when used in place of or with names.

14. Names of schools, clubs, organizations, and buildings.

15. Names of streets, avenues, boulevards, roads, and rural routes.

16. Names of cities, towns, counties, states, countries, and continents.

17. Names of rivers, oceans, mountains, and regions (the South).

18. Names of days, months, holidays, and other special days.

19. Names of businesses and special products.

20. Names of languages, nationalities, and special groups.

21. Names of political parties.

22. Names of government departments.

23. Names for the Deity.

24. Names of churches and religious denominations.

25. Names of historical events and documents.

26. Names of airlines, ships, and railroads.

27. Names of magazines and newspapers.

28. The first word of a head and a subhead in outlines.

29. The first word after a strong interjection.

RULES FOR PUNCTUATION

A **period** is used:
1. At the end of a declarative sentence.
2. At the end of an imperative sentence.
3. After numerals and letters in outlines.
4. At the end of a business request stated in question form.
5. After an abbreviation or an initial.

A **question mark** is used:
1. At the end of an interrogative sentence.
2. Inside parentheses after a date or statement to show doubt.

An **exclamation point** is used:
1. At the end of an exclamatory sentence.
2. After a very strong interjection.
3. At the end of an imperative sentence that exclaims.

A **comma** is used:
1. To separate items in a series.
2. To separate adjectives of equal value.
3. To separate a direct quotation from the rest of a sentence.
4. To separate the day of the month from the year.
5. To separate the names of a city and a state.
6. To separate a name from a title (David Bird, President).
7. To set off adjectives in an appositive position.
8. To set off introductory words like *no* and *now*.
9. To set off transitional words like *however*, *moreover*, and *nevertheless*.
10. To set off a name used in direct address.
11. To set off a nonrestrictive adjective clause.
12. To set off most words used in apposition.
13. After the greeting in a friendly letter.
14. After the closing in any letter.
15. After a last name preceding a first name.
16. After a mild interjection within a sentence.
17. After an introductory adverbial clause.
18. After an introductory participial phrase.
19. Before the conjunction in a compound sentence.
20. Whenever necessary to make meaning clear.

An **apostrophe** is used:
1. To show possession.
2. In contractions.
3. To form plurals of letters, figures, signs, and words.

Quotation marks are used:
1. To enclose the exact words of a speaker.
2. Around titles of short plays, short stories, short poems, chapter titles, and songs.

A **colon** is used:
1. In writing time (6:45).
2. To introduce a list.
3. After the greeting in a business letter.
4. In written plays and in other forms of written dialogue, after the name of the character who is speaking.

A **semicolon** is used:
1. To join independent clauses in a compound sentence when a conjunction is not present.
2. To precede a conjunctive adverb (therefore, however, furthermore, etc.) used between the coordinate clauses of a compound sentence.
3. In place of a comma when a more distinct pause is desired.

Underlining is used:
1. Below handwritten or typewritten titles of movies, newspapers, books, magazines, ships, and trains.
2. To set off foreign words and phrases which are not yet part of the English language.

A **hypen** is used:
1. In writing compound numbers.
2. To divide a word at the end of a line.
3. Between parts of a compound adjective preceding a noun.

A **dash** is used:
1. To indicate an abrupt break in thought or structure.
2. To indicate a parenthetical or explanatory phrase or clause.
3. Between numbers in a page reference.

Parentheses are used:
1. To enclose material that is supplementary, explanatory, or interpretive.
2. To enclose a question mark after a date or a statement to show doubt.
3. To enclose an author's insertion or comment.

SELECTED GRAMMAR TERMS

Abstract Noun - a noun that names things which do not have a physical substance. Example: *compassion*.

Active Voice - a verb which expresses action and can take a direct object. Example: I *threw* the ball.

Adjective - a word that modifies a noun, or a pronoun Example: the *white* ball.

Adverb - a word that modifies a verb, an adjective, or another adverb. Example: Go *slowly*.

Antecedent - the word, phrase, or clause to which a relative pronoun refers. A pronoun must agree with its antecedent in number. Example: *Erin* gave me his ball.

Articles - the adjectives *a*, *an*, and *the*.

Auxiliary Verb -a verb that accompanies another verb to show tense, mood, or voice. Example: She *has* gone.

Clause - a group of words that contains a subject and a predicate, and forms part of a compound or complex sentence. Example: *After I left, she called.*

Collective Noun - a noun that denotes a collection of persons or things regarded as a unit; usually takes a singular verb. Example: The *committee* chooses its own chairman.

Common Noun - a noun that indicates any one of a class of persons, places, or things. Examples: *boy; town; ball.*

Comparative Adjective - an adjective form (ending in —*er* or adding the word *more* before the word) used when two persons or things are compared. Example: This apple is *smaller* and more *delicious* than that one.

Complex Sentence - a sentence containing one independent clause and one or more dependent clauses. Example: *I went to town to shop, but found that all the stores were closed.*

Compound Sentence - a sentence containing two or more independent clauses joined by a conjunction. Example: *I called my friend, and we talked for an hour.*

Compound-Complex Sentence - a sentence that has two or more independent clauses and at least one dependent or subordinate clause. Example: *When she opened the door, there was no one on the porch, and the street was empty, too.*

Concrete Noun - a noun that names a physical, visible, or tangible item. Example: *airplane*.

Conjunction - a word that connects words, phrases, or clauses. Example: I like toast *and* jam.

Coordinating Conjunction - a conjunction used to connect two independent clauses. Example: He grinned, *and* I giggled.

Correlative Conjunction - conjunctions which are used in pairs. Example: *Neither* Alan *nor* Amy will go.

Dependent (or Subordinate) Clause - a clause that functions as a noun, adjective, or adverb within a sentence, but cannot stand alone.
Example: *What she said* was true.

Direct Object - the noun, pronoun, or noun phrase in a sentence which receives the action of a transitive verb.
Example: I threw the *ball.*

Gerund - a verb form ending in *-ing,* usually used as a noun.
Example: *Skiing* is fun.

Indefinite Pronoun - a pronoun that does not specify the identity of its object.
Example: *Anyone* can come.

Independent Clause - a clause which contains at least a subject and a predicate, and is capable of standing alone.
Example: *I went to the store.*

Indirect Object - the noun, pronoun, or noun phrase named as the one to whom or for whom action involving a direct object is done.
Example: He gave *me* the paper.

Infinitive - a non-inflected verb form usually preceded by *to,* used as a noun, adjective, or adverb.
Example: *To run* fast is fun.

Intensive Pronoun - a pronoun which is used for emphasis.
Example: I *myself* saw it.

Interjection - an exclamatory word or phrase.
Example: *Hey! Look out!*

Intransitive Verb - a verb that does not require an object.
Example: She *learns* easily.

Linking Verb - a verb that can be followed by an adjective that modifies the subject.
Example: Randy *is* tall.

Modify - to qualify or limit the meaning of.
Example: *very* small.

Noun - a word that names a person, place, or thing.
Examples: *girl, city, hat.*

Paragraph - a distinct division within a written work that may consist of several sentences or just one, that expresses something relevant to the whole work but is complete within itself.

Passive Voice - a verb which expresses state of being and cannot take a direct object.
Example: He *was asked* to leave.

Past Tense - a verb form that expresses action or condition that occurred in the past.
Example: Yesterday I *went* to town.

Personal Pronoun - a pronoun that denotes the speaker, person spoken to, or person spoken about.
Example: *You* can find it.

Positive Adjective - an adjective form used to assign a quality to the word it modifies.
Example: the *fast* car.

Possessive Pronoun - a pronoun that shows possession.
Example: That car is *mine.*

Predicate - the portion of a sentence or clause that tells something about the subject, consisting of a verb and possibly including objects, modifiers, and/or verb complements.

Predicate Adjective - an adjective that refers to, describes, or limits the subject of a sentence.
Example: The rock is *heavy*.

Predicate Nominative - a noun following a form of the verb *to be* in a sentence which modifies the subject.
Example: She is *Alicia*.

Preposition - a word that shows relationship (often between verbs and nouns or nouns and nouns) and takes an object.
Example: Put it *on* the table.

Prepositional Phrase - a group of words in a sentence that includes a preposition and its object, along with any modifiers of the object.
Example: Put it *on the first table*.

Present Tense - a verb form that expresses current time.
Example: I *am* here.

Pronoun - a word that takes the place of a noun.
Example: *I; you; she; it; he*.

Proper Noun - a noun that names a particular person, place, or thing, and is capitalized.
Examples: *Omaha; Jenny*.

Reflexive Pronoun - a pronoun that ends in *-self* or *-selves;* used to point the action back to the subject.
Example: You will hurt *yourself*.

Relative Pronoun - a pronoun that shows a relationship.
Example: It was he *who* did it.

Run-On (or Fused) Sentence - a sentence in which two complete sentences are run together with no punctuation to separate them.
Example: *I went to the movie I ate some popcorn*.

Sentence - a basic unit of language which must contain a subject and a predicate.
Example: *I went to the movie*.

Subject - a word or phrase in a sentence that is the doer of the action, or receives the action (in passive voice), or which is described; must agree in number with the predicate.
Example: *Margaret* was there.

Subjunctive (or Conditional) Mood - a set of verb forms used to express contingent or hypothetical action, usually introduced by *if, that,* etc., and always taking the plural form of the verb.
Example: *If I were you, I'd go*.

Superlative Adjective - an adjective form (ending in *-est* or adding the word *most* before the word) used when three or more things are involved in a comparison.
Example: This is the *slowest* of all cars.

Transitive - a verb which can take an object within a sentence.
Example: He *threw* the ball.

Verb - a word that shows action, state of being, or occurrence.
Examples: *run; is; find*.

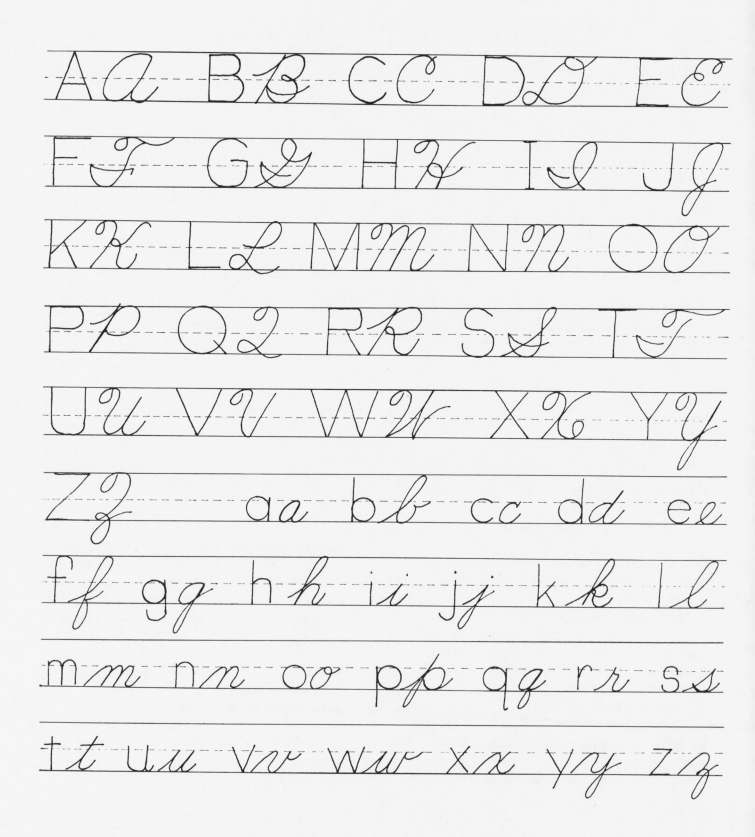

FORMS FOR LETTER WRITING

BLOCK STYLE

(your street address) _____ *
(your city, state, and Zip) _____ *   Heading
(the date) _____

(addressee's name) _____
(company's name) _____   Inside Address
(company's street address) _____
(company's city, state, and Zip) _____

_____ :   Greeting/Salutation

_____
_____
_____
_____   Body of Letter
_____
_____
_____

_____ ,   Complimentary Close

(your handwritten name) _____   Signature
(your typed name) _____

* Do not include if you are using paper with a letterhead on it.

MODIFIED BLOCK

Heading

                        (your street address) _____ *
                        (your city, state, and Zip) _____ *
                        (the date) _____

(addressee's name) _____
(company's name) _____   Inside Address
(company's street address) _____
(company's city, state, and Zip) _____

_____ :   Greeting/Salutation

_____
_____
_____
_____   Body of Letter
_____
_____
_____

Complimentary Close   _____ ,

Signature   (your handwritten name) _____
                             (your typed name) _____

* Do not include if you are using paper with a letterhead on it.

MODIFIED SEMIBLOCK

Heading

                        (your street address) _____ *
                        (your city, state, and Zip) _____ *
                        (the date) _____

(addressee's name) _____
(company's name) _____   Inside Address
(company's street address) _____
(company's city, state, and Zip) _____

_____ :   Greeting/Salutation

_____
_____
_____   Body of Letter
_____
_____
_____

Complimentary Close   _____ ,

Signature   (your handwritten name) _____
                             (your typed name) _____

* Do not include if you are using paper with a letterhead on it.

FRIENDLY LETTER

Heading

                        (your street address) _____ *
                        (your city, state, and Zip) _____ *
                        (the date) _____

_____ ,   Greeting/Salutation

_____
_____   Body of Letter
_____
_____
_____
_____
_____
_____

Complimentary Close   _____ ,

Signature   _____

* Do not include if this information is printed or engraved on your stationery.

37

PRIMARY EDITOR'S GUIDE

1. Who will read my work?

2. Will they find it interesting?

3. Have I spelled all words correctly?
    (Check words you aren't sure about. Ask a good speller to read and check your spelling for you.)

4. Have I used correct grammar and punctuation? Are periods, commas, question marks, quotation marks, exclamation points, and capital letters in the right places?
    (Reread to check yourself; then, ask a friend to double-check for you.)

5. Are my ideas in the right order?
    (Did I tell the first thing first and the others in sequence as they happened?)

6. Have I used words that my readers will understand easily?

7. Have I used interesting words that the reader will enjoy?

8. Have I overused any words or phrases?

9. Have I used any examples or illustrations to help explain my ideas?

10. Have I omitted any important details or information?

11. Have I said what I really think, and not just what I think my friends or my teacher would expect me to say?

12. Is my ending good? Does it really end the story or idea?

13. Is my handwriting clear and easy to read?

14. Have I used my own ideas and opinions?

15. What is special about my writing that will make my readers be glad that they read it?

INTERMEDIATE EDITOR'S GUIDE

1. Have I visualized my reader? Do I understand what interests him or her?

2. Have I given careful attention to grammar, spelling, and punctuation so that my reader will experience no confusion in understanding my message?
    (Proofread your writing, and then have a person skilled in proofreading recheck for technical errors.)

3. Have I expressed my thoughts in logical, sequential order?
    (Number the main ideas to check this.)

4. Have I used plain, simple words that are comfortable for my reader to read?

5. Have I used these plain, simple words in a way that will interest my reader?

6. Have I deleted unnecessary words or phrases?

7. Have I deleted unrelated or irrelevant matter?
    (Underline sentences or phrases that may not relate.)

8. Have I omitted any vital or important details or information?

9. Have I avoided overworked words, phrases, and cliche's?
    (Cross out any you have used, and write a better synonym above each.)

10. Have I used the most active and "alive" words possible to express my ideas?
    (Look at each adjective and adverb. Ask yourself if there is a better, more interesting, more picturesque, or more precise word you might substitute.)

11. Have I used illustrations or examples to reinforce main ideas?
    (Make an X at places where such entries may be helpful.)

12. Have I created added interest by interspersing figures of speech, forceful repetition, or exclamations into ordinary, declarative thought? (Count the number of question marks, exclamation points, quotation marks, and figures of speech you have used.)

13. Have I expressed what I honestly feel or believe, or have I been more concerned about what my teacher or my peers will think?
    (Use tact and sensitivity in expressing negative or unpopular feelings or ideas, but do not sacrifice clarity or effectiveness.)

14. Is my writing clear, neat, and easy to read?

15. Have I referred to the beginning in the ending and left my reader with an idea to ponder? Have I said anything to cause my reader to reconsider the subject?

EDITING SKILLS CHECKLIST

Student's Name	Grade	Date	Teacher's Name

SKILLS   **NOTES**

___ Substituting stronger (more colorful, more specific) words

___ Replacing inactive verbs with active ones

___ Eliminating redundancies

___ Rearranging words within a sentence

___ Expanding sentences to include more detail

___ Adding sentences to give more detail to a paragraph

___ Rearranging sentences for better clarity

___ Rearranging sentences for better sequencing

___ Rearranging sentences for a different meaning or sound

___ Making stronger titles

___ Changing endings

___ Creating smashing beginnings

___ Eliminating repetitive ideas or words

___ Eliminating unnecessary ideas or words

___ Breaking long sentences into shorter ones

___ Deciding if the written piece accomplishes the purpose

___ Adding words or phrases that create a certain mood, feeling

___ Varying sentence length and structure within a piece

___ Strengthening and varying transitions

___ Eliminating overused words, phrases, and cliche's

___ Replacing ordinary words with more interesting ones

___ Including words that convince

___ Adapting the content and form to a different audience

___ Changing outcomes by rearranging ideas

___ Adding dialogue to the piece

___ Adding understatement, exaggeration, foreshadowing, or irony to the piece

___ Including figures of speech

___ Varying rhymes and rhythms

___ Varying punctuation

___ Examining pieces for bias

___ Examining pieces for clarity

___ Examining pieces for effectiveness

___ Examining pieces to see that they appeal to the intended reader

PROOFREADERS' MARKS

Instruction	Mark in Margin	Mark in Type	Corrected Type
Delete	ℯ	the ~~good~~ word	the word
Insert indicated material	good	the ⋀word	the good word
Let it stand	(stet)	the ~~good~~ word	the good word
Make capital	(cap)	the ̲w̲ord	the Word
Make lower case	(lc)	╱The Word	the Word
Set in small capitals	(sc)	See ̲word̲.	See WORD.
Set in italic type	(ital)	The word is ̲word̲.	The word is *word*.
Set in roman type	(rom)	the ⟨word⟩	the word
Set in boldface type	(bf)	the entry word̰	the entry **word**
Set in lightface type	(lf)	the entry ⟨word⟩	the entry word
Transpose	(tr)	the ⟨word⟩⟨good⟩	the good word
Close up space	⌒	the wo⌒rd	the word
Delete and close up space	⌒ℯ	the w⌒o̸rd	the word
Spell out	(sp)	②words	two words
Insert: space	#	the⎮word	the word
period	⊙	This is the word⋀	This is the word.
comma	⋏	words⋀words, words	words, words, words
hyphen	⌢=⌒╱⌒ ≠ ⌒	word⋀for⋀word test	word-for-word test
colon	⊙⊙	The following words⋀	The following words:
semicolon	⌢;	Scan the words⋀skim the words.	Scan the words; skim the words.
apostrophe	⌄	John✗s words	John's words

41

Mark	Symbol	Marked copy	Corrected copy
quotation marks	$\overset{\smile}{\diagup}/\overset{\smile}{\diagup}/$	the word word	the word "word"
parentheses	$(/)/$	The word word is in parentheses.	The word (word) is in parentheses.
brackets	$[/]/$	He read from the Word the Bible.	He read from the Word [the Bible].
en dash	$\frac{\mathrm{l}}{\mathrm{N}}$	1964 1972	1964–1972
em dash	$\frac{\mathrm{l}}{\mathrm{M}}/\frac{\mathrm{l}}{\mathrm{M}}/$	The dictionary how often it is needed belongs in every home.	The dictionary—how often it is needed— belongs in every home.
superior type	$\overset{2}{\vee}$	2 = 4	$2^2 = 4$
inferior type	$\overset{}{\wedge}2$	H O	H_2O
asterisk	$\overset{*}{\vee}$	word	word*
dagger	†	a word	a word†
double dagger	‡	words and words	words and words‡
section symbol	§	Book Reviews	§Book Reviews
virgule	/	either or	either/or
Start paragraph	¶	"Where is it?" "It's on the shelf."	"Where is it?" "It's on the shelf."
Run in	(run in)	The entry word is printed in boldface. The pronunciation follows.	The entry word is printed in boldface. The pronunciation follows.
Turn right side up	↺	the word	the word
Move left	⊏	⊏ the word	the word
Move right	⊐	the word	the word
Move up	⊓	the word	the word
Move down	⊔	the word	the word
Align	‖	the word the word the word	the word the word the word
Straighten line	⹀	the word	the word
Wrong font	(wf)	the word	the word
Broken type	×	the word	the word

SELECTED WRITERS' AIDS

Dictionaries
The American Heritage Dictionary of the English Language
   W. Morris, ed. American Heritage Pub. Co./Houghton Mifflin
Bernstein's Reverse Dictionary
   Bernstein. The New York Times Book Co.
The Complete Rhyming Dictionary
   C. Wood, ed. Doubleday & Co.
Everyman's Dictionary of Abbreviations
   J. Paxton. Barnes & Noble.
Macmillan Dictionary for Children
   P. R. Winant, sup. ed. Macmillan Pub. Co., Inc.
New Rhyming Dictionary and Poet's Handbook
   Johnson. Harper & Row.
Webster's New World Speller/Divider
   _____ . W. Collins, Pub.
Webster's Ninth New Collegiate Dictionary
   Merriam-Webster, Inc.

Grammar and Usage
The Art of Styling Sentences
   Waddel, Esch, and Walker. Barrons.
The Complete Letter Writer
   N. H. and S. K. Mager. Simon & Schuster.
The Golden Book on Writing
   Lambuth. Penguin.
Instant Vocabulary
   Ehrlich. Pocket Books.
The New York Times Manual of Style and Usage
   L. Jordan, ed. Quadrangle/The New York Times Book Co.
Punctuate It Right!
   H. Shaw. Harper & Row.
Use the Right Word
   S. I. Hayakawa, ed. The Reader's Digest Assn., Inc.
Word Watcher's Handbook
   Martin. David McKay Co., Inc.
Write It Right
   Kredenser. Barnes & Noble.
The Young Writer's Handbook
   Susan and Stephen Tchudi. Aladdin Books/Macmillan Pub. Co.

Quotations and Slang
Bartlett's Familiar Quotations
   E. M. Beck, ed. Little, Brown & Co.
Dictionary of American Slang
   Wentworth and Flexner. Simon & Schuster.
The International Thesaurus of Quotations
   R. T. Tripp, comp. Thomas Y. Crowell Co.

Thesauri
A Basic Dictionary of Synonyms and Antonyms
   L. Urdang. Elsevier/Nelson Books.
The Clear and Simple Thesaurus Dictionary
   Wittles and Greisman. Grosset & Dunlap.
Roget's International Thesaurus, 3rd ed.
   Rev. by R. L. Chapman. Harper & Row.
The Word Finder
   E. J. Fluck, et al. Rodale Press.

WRITING SKILLS CHECKLIST

Student's Name	Grade	Date	Teacher's Name

I. USING WORDS AND PHRASES

PARTS OF SPEECH

____ Nouns
____ Verbs
____ Adjectives
____ Adverbs
____ Words Used as More Than One Part of Speech

WORD USAGE

____ Synonyms, Antonyms, Homonyms
____ Multiple Meanings
____ Comparisons
____ Plurals and Possessives
____ Preciseness
____ Abbreviations and Contractions
____ Avoid Cliche's

VOCABULARY DEVELOPMENT

____ Internalizing Word Meanings
____ Finding Alternatives for Overworked Words
____ Using Jargon and Current Vocabulary

II. USING TECHNICAL WRITING SKILLS

USING PUNCTUATION MARKS

____ End Punctuation
____ Commas
____ Apostrophes
____ Quotation Marks
____ Colons and Semicolons
____ Parentheses

___ **USING CAPITAL LETTERS**

___ **SPELLING**

WRITING SENTENCES

___ Four Kinds of Sentences
___ Writing a Good Sentence
___ Fragments, Complete Sentences
___ Run-On Sentences
___ Subject-Verb Agreement
___ Sentence Structure
___ Parallel Construction

WRITING PARAGRAPHS

___ Writing Topic Sentences
___ Organizing a Paragraph

III. COMPOSITION AND ORIGINAL WRITING

COLLECTING AND ORGANIZING IDEAS

___ Using a Variety of Resources
___ Sequencing Thoughts
___ Note Taking, Summarizing
___ Paraphrasing
___ Précis Writing

USING FIGURATIVE LANGUAGE

___ Metaphors and Similes
___ Personification, Alliteration, Onomatopoeia

USING SPECIAL LITERARY DEVICES

___ Sensory Appeal
___ Point of View
___ Puns
___ Emotional Appeal
___ Unusual Perspective
___ Imagery, Mood, Parody, Irony, Hyperbole

USING PROSE FORMS

____ Characterization
____ Description
____ Dialogue
____ Narrative
____ News Reporting, Editorials

USING POETIC FORMS

____ Rhymed (couplets, rhyme schemes, etc.)
____ Unrhymed (haiku, cinquain, quatrain, free verse, etc.)

____ **WRITING TITLES, CAPTIONS, AND LABELS**

____ **EDITING AND PROOFREADING**

IV. WRITING FOR EVERYDAY LIVING

LETTER WRITING

____ Friendly, Social Notes, Business
____ Envelopes

INFORMATIONAL AND INSTRUCTIONAL WRITING

____ Graphs and Diagrams
____ Signs and Posters
____ Pictorial Directions
____ Procedural Directions
____ Geographical Directions

COMPLETING INFORMATIONAL FORMS

____ Identification and Registration
____ Applications
____ Contracts
____ Order Blanks

ORGANIZING AND RECORDING FACTUAL DATA

____ Record Keeping and Inventories
____ Memos
____ Biographies
____ Bibliographies
____ Checks and Deposits
____ Journals and Diaries
____ Lists
____ Ads
____ Reports

A CHECKLIST TO ENCOURAGE CREATIVE WRITING

Try something new each week.

Write weekly goals and evaluate goal achievement regularly.	
Think of one thing that bothers you and write a proposed plan for changing it.	
Read one "easy" book and one "hard" book and write a brief summary of each.	
Keep a daily journal.	
Talk to three people about a topic that interests you. Compare and contrast their opinions in paragraph form.	
Read a daily newspaper and write a synopsis of an interesting article.	
Read two different newspaper accounts of a news event and write a comparison of the two accounts.	
Read an editorial from the Sunday newspaper. Question the position taken and write your own ideas concerning the issue at hand.	
Poll your classmates on a topic of current interest. Graph or chart the results.	
Add ten new words to your vocabulary.	
Write an original poem, story, or song. Reread it a day later and then try to make it more interesting or exciting.	
Learn something new about a city or country and then share your findings in an original travel brochure.	
Study the life and times of a famous person and write a brief biography for someone who might never have heard of him or her.	
Select a subject to research. Use three different sources and summarize your findings.	
Participate in a brainstorming session.	
Select one current event from the news and predict what will happen concerning this current event in the next seven days. Write your prediction and check it against the actual happenings at the end of the week.	
Keep a sequential record of some aspect of your environment (growth of a plant, the weather, etc.). Review the record and note any changes as well as the causes and effects of those changes.	
Work a word puzzle.	
Make up a word puzzle and ask someone to solve it.	
Write an evaluation of your progress in school.	
Make something out of three-dimensional materials and write a detailed description of the object.	
Make a list of things to do next week — some practical and some just-for-fun things.	
Share an imaginative, unusual, or "way-out" idea with someone. Record their reaction.	

WORDS AND PHRASES
THAT BREED AND AID IDEA PRODUCTION

illustrate	diagram	substitute	extrude	rearrange
subtract	minimize	integrate	transpose	flatten
fallen	abstract	eliminate	unify	modify
adapt	add	segregate	reverse	invert
symbolize	translate	stretch	separate	distort
rotate	elaborate	dissect	combine	squeeze
complement	freeze	thicken	lighten	relate
multiply	decrease	regulate	turn	convert
increase	shift	modulate	mold	stain
alter	variegate	mutate	revolutionize	arrange
modernize	recast	affirm	edit	vary
superimpose	patch	adjust	impair	mar
revamp	strain	twist	adulterate	dye
bend	cover	mask	disguise	shuffle
denature	transfigure	reorder	crossbreed	process
conceal	organize	extend	magnify	

Name as many things as possible that _____ .

How many ways can you think of to _____ ?

What are all the meanings you can think of for _____ ?

How many different ways can you express _____ ?

List every fact you can think of related to _____ .

The answer is _____ . List as many questions as you can think of for which that is the answer.

What are all the words you could use instead of _____ ?

How many different ways can you show _____ ?

How would this look to a _____ ?

What would happen if _____ ?

How is _____ like _____ ?

How would you feel if _____ ?

How would this be viewed by _____ ?

How would someone else feel if you _____ ?

WHAT WOULD YOU DO?

Write two complete sentences suggesting two ways to handle each of the following situations — one proposing a poor solution, and one proposing a good solution.

1. You were being chased by an elephant.
2. You received a nasty letter from a stranger.
3. You inherited a million dollars.
4. You met a fire-eating dragon face to face.
5. You found yourself in a haunted house at midnight.
6. The principal asked you to take charge of the entire school for a day.
7. Someone handed you three double-dip ice cream cones at noon on a hot day.
8. You found yourself lost in a deep, dark forest.
9. You had to walk to school during a rain shower with no umbrella or raincoat.
10. The only food you had to eat for a week was asparagus.
11. Someone left a tiny puppy in a basket on your doorstep.
12. You were accused of a crime you didn't commit.
13. You found a wallet containing three one hundred dollar bills on the sidewalk.
14. A fairy godmother suddenly appeared to grant one wish for you.
15. Your best friend was quarantined with a contagious disease for a month.
16. You were asked to spend a week on tour with the president of your country.
17. All the books in the world were destroyed.
18. You broke out in a rash from head to toe on the doctor's day off.
19. You had to cross a river without a bridge or a boat.
20. You met a real leprechaun at midnight on St. Patrick's Day.
21. It rained continuously for forty days and forty nights.
22. While fishing in a pond near your home, you hooked an alligator.
23. Someone delivered sixty-nine crates of ripe tomatoes to your house.
24. A neighbor gave you a map of the neighborhood with an X marking the spot where a hidden treasure was supposedly buried.
25. You opened the kitchen door early one morning to find a huge banner proclaiming you "Citizen of the Day."
26. After a sudden rain, you followed a rainbow to its end and found a real pot of gold with instructions to spend all of the gold before nightfall.
27. The king of a very important country asked you to live in the palace and be his chief assistant for one year.
28. You found yourself responsible for planning an after-school educational program for all the children under twelve in your town.
29. Suppose that none of the trees in the world had names and you had to write a book naming and describing each tree.
30. You awakened at your school desk and were told that you had been asleep for six weeks.
31. Someone gave you a magic airplane ticket with which you could travel to any place in the world. There was one catch — it was a one-way ticket!
32. You were performing on a stage before thousands of people and your trousers fell down.
33. You were making an emergency trip down a two-lane mountain road, and you found a huge boulder blocking the road.

LIST MAKING—A SPRINGBOARD TO DIVERGENT THINKING

Make a list of:

1. Twenty ways to move a heavy box from one room to another.
2. Fifteen uses for a potato masher (other than mashing potatoes).
3. Forty-nine four-syllable words.
4. Sixteen uses for or things to do with an old newspaper.
5. Foods from countries other than your own (list the country for each).
6. Six places in your own community where you could go to observe animals in their natural habitats.
7. The full names of sixteen people over seventy years old.
8. Ten toys that would be safe for a one-year-old baby.
9. Five ways to put out a fire.
10. Twenty-nine minerals.
11. Fifty-two vegetables (two that begin with each letter in the alphabet).
12. Fourteen words that name something to be worn on a person's head.
13. Twenty-two well-known bodies of water.
14. Twelve ways to save money.
15. Sixteen things with which to write.
16. Twelve holidays (give the date and the symbol(s) for each).
17. Ten sources you could use to locate information on Antarctica.
18. Authors of books you have read during the past three months.
19. Forty color words.
20. Twenty uses for a lemon.
21. Twenty-four analogies.
22. Fifteen kinds of boats.
23. Fifteen things to wear on your feet.
24. Ten things that could be used to hold papers together.
25. Thirty-six musical instruments.
26. Six ways to cook tomatoes.
27. One hundred and two parts of an automobile.
28. Nine ways to tell time.
29. Twenty-one careers in the world of the theater.
30. Twenty-six cities west of the Mississippi River.
31. Ten kinds of beans.
32. Eight words that mean "cold."
33. Forty-five varieties of trees.
34. Eight ways to cook without electricity.
35. Roman numerals from one through one hundred. Multiply each number on your list by ten, and write the products in Roman numerals.
36. Six places where you could find the correct spellings of the continents.
37. Fifty-nine kinds of sandwiches.
38. A dozen ways to use eggshells.
39. The ten most recent chief executives of your country.
40. Seventy-seven words that begin with the letter "s" (without using the dictionary).
41. The full name of every teacher you have ever had.
42. Seven different kinds of grain used to make bread.
43. The ten largest cities in the world.

THINK OF TEN ORIGINAL, NEVER-BEFORE-THOUGHT-OF . . .

ways to report on a book

ways to serve potatoes

titles for patriotic songs

uses for ice cubes

gifts to make for special occasions

ideas for parties

names for a pet fish

ways to say, "I love you."

ways to say, "I'm sorry."

recipes using chocolate

names for romantic novels

ideas for short stories

uses for last year's calendar

ways to help people less fortunate than yourself

games to play with three other people

four-line rhymes

words and their definitions

holidays

subjects to study in school

ways to honor senior citizens

educational toys

colors

substitutes for shoes

themes for amusement parks

Halloween costumes

uses for peach pits

ways to paint a picture

uses for marshmallows

places to get married

uses for litter

ways to conserve natural resources

reasons to clean your room

water sports

uses for paper clips

WAYS TO ORGANIZE INFORMATION

Synopsize

Make a card file

Code

Categorize

Diagram

Outline

List

Map

Catalog

Schedule

Index

Keep a journal

Make a table

Make a sketch

Create a layout

Make a file

Serialize

Alphabetize

Order numerically

Classify by theme or subject

Order qualitatively

Make a time line

Order sequentially

Make a mock-up

Color code

Make a chart

Make a graph

Order according to the
references used

Write a report

Record information on tape

Take photographs

Order quantitatively

Order chronologically

Order according
to importance

Write a paragraph

Take notes

Organize according
to similarities

Organize according
to differences

Organize according
to author

Draw pictures

ANALOGIES

Five is to ten as eight is to sixteen.
Bake is to cake as broil is to meat.
Octopus is to ocean as tiger is to jungle.
Add is to subtract as multiply is to divide.
Sing is to voice as dance is to legs.
Ink is to pen as paint is to brush.
Brush is to comb as fork is to knife.
Milk is to cereal as syrup is to pancakes.
Bacon is to eggs as jelly is to toast.
Goose is to gander as cow is to bull.
Channel is to TV as station is to radio.
Down is to up as low is to high.
Elbow is to arm as knee is to leg.
Ankle is to foot as wrist is to hand.
Top is to bottom as back is to front.
Yellow is to lemon as green is to celery.
Hour is to day as week is to month.
Cup is to drink as plate is to eat.
Mare is to colt as cow is to calf.
Listen is to hear as look is to see.
Bee is to hive as bird is to nest.
Gold is to mine as oil is to well.
Pie is to dessert as lettuce is to salad.
Gasoline is to car as diesel is to train.
Tomato is to fruit as corn is to vegetable.
Bus is to driver as ship is to captain.
Nail is to finger as hair is to head.
Music is to radio as program is to TV.
Big is to little as large is to small.
Good is to bad as day is to night.
Chocolate is to vanilla as dark is to light.
Shirt is to pants as sock is to shoe.
Few is to many as some is to all.
Smoke is to fire as rain is to clouds.
On is to off as start is to stop.
Go is to green as stop is to red.
Toe is to foot as finger is to hand.
A portrait is to a person as a map is to a city.
Teacher is to student as coach is to player.
Centimeter is to meter as inch is to yard.

A ship is to the sea as a plane is to the air.
Ring is to finger as watch is to arm.
Ounce is to pound as gram is to kilogram.
Second is to minute as minute is to hour.
Quart is to ounce as liter is to milliliter.
Writer is to book as illustrator is to picture.
Brother is to boy as sister is to girl.
Cut is to scissors as slice is to knife.
Water is to plant as food is to people.
Napkin is to lap as tablecloth is to table.
Capital is to city as capitol is to building.
Sugar is to sweet as lemon is to sour.
Stove is to cook as car is to ride.
Dresses are to ladies as booties are to babies.
Bed is to bedroom as bathtub is to bathroom.
A den is to a fox as a cave is to a bat.
A chick is to a hen as a kitten is to a cat.
A princess is to a prince as a queen is to a king.
A lady is to a gentleman as a woman is to a man.
Eye is to see as ear is to hear.
A teacher is to a classroom as a principal is to a school.
Commercial is to TV as ad is to newspaper.
Horizontal is to the ground as vertical is to a tree.
Enter is to exit as come is to go.
Boat is to lake as ship is to ocean.
A day is to a week as a month is to a year.
A cavity is to a dentist as a mystery is to a detective.
An insect is to little as a hippopotamus is to big.
Stone is to hard as sand is to soft.
Meow is to a cat as hiss is to a snake.
A cage is to a parakeet as an aquarium is to a fish.
A bat is to a ball as a screwdriver is to a screw.
Clothing is to people as fur is to animals.
Lead is to a pencil as tobacco is to a pipe.
Hamburger is to French fries as steak is to baked potatoes.
A page is to a book as a piece is to a puzzle.
Laugh is to cry as smile is to frown.
A clock is to time as a thermometer is to temperature.
Sun is to solar energy as water power is to electricity.
Air conditioning is to summer as heating is to winter.
A whale is to a minnow as an elephant is to a mouse.
Job is to work as party is to play.
Crayons are to drawing as paintbrushes are to painting.
Salt water is to ocean as fresh water is to lake.

PUNS

A little fish asked the leviathan, "Are you ill?" The leviathan replied, "No, I'm whale."

Did you hear about the smart pole vaulter who really had the jump on things?

A silly lady is a dumb belle.

A swimming animal that barks is a dog fish.

"Dash it all!" exclaimed the runner.

The ruling animal is the reign-deer.

An octopus is a cat with eight sides.

The scissors-happy film director said, "Cut! Cut!"

When asked why he was being spanked, the confused child said, "Beats me!"

A lost puppy is a dog gone.

"Don't drop the eggs," cracked the grocer.

Did you hear about the snobbish robbery victim who was really stuck up?

"I love all people," said the cannibal.

If your refrigerator is running, you should try to catch it!

A well is a deep subject.

...as the lawyer said, "Just in case."

Said the golfer as he searched for his lost ball, "I don't know where I putt it."

A kindergarten teacher tries to make little things count.

The grizzly said, "I can't bear it any more."

"I always let things slide," said the trombonist.

The dentist said, "My occupation is very filling."

"Could you please hurry?" said the man on his way to the cleaners. "I have a pressing engagement."

My cookbook certainly is exciting — it contains such stirring events.

A teacher without students has no class.

The baker really got a rise out of that.

The largest ants in the world are gi-ants.

The butcher is really a cut above the rest.

"See you around," said the circle.

When the salesman left, he said, "Buy, buy!"

The strangest creature I've ever seen is a spelling bee.

The author said, "Write on!"

A sign hanging on an old boat read: "For sail."

The tailor said, "Will this outfit suit you, sir?"

A clockmaker always works overtime.

Another name for an angrily rising ocean is an emergent sea (emergency).

"I want no part of that," said the bald man.

A barber runs a clip joint.

"Hand it over," said the manicurist.

The shoemaker said, "That boot really has sole!"

The principal part of a lion is its mane.

The night watchman said, "I've never done a day's work."

Dawn breaks but never falls.

The astronomer said, "My business is looking up."

I thought the Dracula movie was a pain in the neck.

The farmer said, "Sow what?"

He could be a wonderful pianist except for two things — his hands.

A demon's favorite dessert is devil's food cake.

The seamstress said, "You're sew right!"

This horn isn't broken — it just doesn't give a hoot!

When the nuclear scientist went on vacation, he left a sign on his door that read, "Gone fission."

The surgeon said, "I'll keep you in stitches."

Did you hear about the clergyman who wanted to make a parson-to-parson call?

If you stuck your head in a washing machine, you'd get brainwashed.

Niagara Falls but never breaks.

Did you hear about the wolf that got trapped in the laundry and became a wash and werewolf?

STORY STARTERS

The famous ballerina leaped into the air . . .

A huge, black bear lumbered toward the highway . . .

Out of the darkness and into the campfire's light came . . .

Please don't say . . .

In magnificent splendor . . .

Suddenly, the sky lit up . . .

A piercing scream broke the stillness . . .

Silly, I know, but . . .

The excitement of the midway became contagious . . .

I don't believe in magic pencils, but . . .

The crocodile opened his jaws wide . . .

Senators should be careful about what they eat . . .

The train roared on into the night . . .

In a split second . . .

The unbelievably beautiful sunset . . .

The fog set in at midday . . .

Snips and snails and sand pails . . .

Miles and miles of forbidding coastline stretched ahead . . .

A house just as desolate as the one before . . .

Where the tornado hit . . .

I'm sorry, but that's just how it is . . .

A ghost was here last night . . .

The boat slowly pulled away from the shore . . .

Man's best friend is . . .

Woman's best friend is . . .

The drill captain roared . . .

As flood waters continued to rise . . .

Right in my own backyard . . .

The driver looked away for just a second . . .

A strange smell came from the swamp . . .

The horizon was covered by a dark cloud . . .

The stone simply would not budge . . .

I became more frightened with every step . . .

Under the giant mushroom . . .

The day the teacher overslept, we . . .

We played this crazy game in which you had to . . .

It all started when . . .

All the kids on the block waited anxiously . . .

The strangest looking dog I've ever seen . ..

The curtains in back of the dusty window parted slowly, and . . .

If I live to be one hundred and four, I'll never . . .

The last bar on the cage gave way, and the lion . . .

The flashlight was shining directly into my tent . . .

The ground began to sink down, down, down . . .

He's been missing for more than two days . . .

Suddenly, the lantern sputtered and went out . . .

A pocket knife is the only clue to . . .

More than anything in the world, she wanted to . . .

Gold! . . .

Under the pillow was a note saying . . .

Gigantic footprints led right up to the . . .

As the band began to play . . .

Caught in the act again! . . .

Please get me out of here . . .

"Open at your own risk" was written on the label . . .

I felt my body shrinking, shrinking . . .

He stuck his hand into the opening and pulled out . . .

The whole town was in an uproar . . .

SELECTED AUTHORS YOUNG WRITERS SHOULD READ

Author	Selected Works	Writing Style Specialty
Alcott, Louisa May	*Little Women* *Little Men*	Characterization
Andersen, Hans Christian	*Andersen's Fairy Tales*	Fantasy
Blume, Judith	*Are You There, God? It's Me, Margaret* *Then Again, Maybe I Won't*	Plot and Sequence
Carroll, Lewis	*Alice's Adventures in Wonderland* *Through the Looking Glass*	Imagery
Cather, Willa	*My Antonia* *Death Comes for the Archbishop*	Characterization; Plot and Sequence
cummings, e. e.	*Tulips and Chimneys* *Poems 1923-1954*	Poetry
Dahl, Roald	*Charlie and the Chocolate Factory*	Plot and Sequence
Dickens, Charles	*A Christmas Carol* *David Copperfield*	Simple ideas, beautifully expressed
Grimm, Jacob and Wilhelm	*Grimms' Fairy Tales*	Fantasy
Halliburton, Richard	*The Royal Road to Romance* *The Flying Carpet*	Journalism
Henry, O.	*The Four Million* *Works of O. Henry*	Short Story Mastery
Keats, Ezra Jack	*The Snowy Day* *Whistle for Willie*	Simple ideas, beautifully expressed
Kipling, Rudyard	*The Jungle Books* *Just So Stories*	Plot and Sequence
Krauss, Ruth	*A Hole Is to Dig* *A Very Special House*	Simple ideas, beautifully expressed
Lear, Edward	*The Complete Nonsense Book* *The Jumblies*	Humor
L'Engle, Madeleine	*A Wrinkle in Time* *Meet the Austins*	Plot and Sequence
Longfellow, Henry W.	*Voices of the Night* *Ballads and Other Poems*	Poetry
McCloskey, Robert	*Make Way for Ducklings* *Time of Wonder*	Plot and Sequence
Milne, A. A.	*When We Were Very Young* *Now We Are Six*	Rhythm

Author	Selected Works	Writing Style Specialty
Nash, Ogden	*Good Intentions* *I'm a Stranger Here Myself*	Humor; Coined Words
Riley, James Whitcomb	*The Old Swimmin' Hole* *'Leven More Poems*	Poetry
Rossetti, Christina	*Sing Song* *Goblin Market and Other Poems*	Poetry
Sandburg, Carl	*Rootabaga Stories* *Wind Song*	Description; Figures of Speech
Sendak, Maurice	*Where the Wild Things Are* *In The Night Kitchen*	Fantasy
Seuss, Dr.	*The Cat in the Hat* *Bartholomew and the Oobleck*	Coined Words; Originality
Silverstein, Shel	*Where the Sidewalk Ends* *Lafcadio*	Divergent Thinking; Humor
Steele, William O.	*The Perilous Road* *Wayah of the Real People*	Plot and Sequence
Stevenson, Robert Louis	*A Child's Garden of Verses*	Poetry
Teasdale, Sara	*Stars Tonight* *Strange Victory*	Lovely Word Usage
Tolkien, J. R. R.	*The Hobbit* *Lord of the Rings*	Creating a believable mythical world
Twain, Mark	*The Adventures of Tom Sawyer* *The Adventures of Huckleberry Finn*	Characterization; Description
Viorst, Judith	*Alexander and the Terrible, Horrible, No Good, Very Bad Day* *Alexander, Who Use to Be Rich Last Sunday*	Brings extraordinary qualities to everyday experiences
White, E. B.	*Charlotte's Web* *The Trumpet of the Swan*	Description; Imagery
Zolotow, Charlotte	*A Father Like That* *When I Have a Son*	Simple ideas, beautifully expressed

IDEAS FOR MIXING WRITING WITH
OTHER CONTENT AREAS

Science

- Make a recipe and menu book containing menus for well-balanced meals.

- Write the life story of a jellyfish or tadpole.

- Write a schedule for the care and feeding of the classroom pet (or your pet at home).

- Make a directory of common diseases. Describe symptoms and cures for each.

- Write a resume' of your qualifications to be class zoo-keeper or plant-tender.

- Write a tribute to your teeth, hair, vocal chords, or muscles.

- Write directions for making a bug-catcher or for preserving animal tracks.

- Write a tongue twister about tongues or tendons.

- After growing crystals, create crystal-shaped poems.

- Prepare a consumer's guide of 50 ways to conserve water.

- When you are studying the universe, write space fantasies.

- Write superstitions. Explain scientifically why each superstition cannot be true.

- Write an index or table of contents for a book on earthquakes, engines, seasons, or electricity.

- Keep data sheets (careful records and notes) on any science experiment. Write a hypothesis before you begin and a summary when you finish.

- Write weather maps to explain weather conditions or any other phenomena that persons long ago might not have understood.

- Create a science calendar. Write and illustrate interesting scientific facts and discoveries on each month's page.

- Compile a booklet of first aid procedures for a school, a home, or a camping trip.

- Write weather poems or personification stories about clouds, hailstones, or tornadoes.

- Write a family album about your own roots. Describe the traits you inherited.

- Write questions for interviewing a geologist, microbiologist, chemist, hematologist, meteorologist, pharmacist, ichthyologist, or physicist.

- Make a directory of plants, land forms, birds, arachnids, or reptiles. Draw 15 or more of each. Label and write distinguishing characteristics.

Math

- Write directions for an original math game that will help players learn math facts.

- Make up jump-rope rhymes using the multiplication facts.

- Write a speech that will convince someone to like math.

- Write imaginative word problems for other people to solve. Use the names of your classmates in the problems.

- Write a love story about a romance between a circle and a trapezoid.

- Write a poem using at least ten math words.

- Write a play about the "Wonderful World of Zero."

- Write the autobiography of a right angle.

- Write a diet for an overweight ton.

- Write a contract between yourself and someone who is buying your bike on time payments.

- Write a menu for a restaurant where a family of four could eat dinner for under $20.00.

- Write couplets that will help you remember your addition facts.

- Make a "no number" booklet telling what the world would be like without numbers.

- Write a song that explains the operation of division.

- Compile your own math dictionary that has clear definitions of the math terms you use.

- Write an ode to the number 17 (or any other) telling why that number is special.

- Make signs, posters and advertising billboards telling about the discounts that will be available at an upcoming sale.

- Make a directory of metric measures. Explain the metric system so that your directory could be used by someone who hasn't learned metrics.

- Write directions telling how to make a cube or any other geometric figure.

- Write a book jacket for your math book . . . or an index . . . or a table of contents.

- Write advertising folders for resorts, camps, cruises, or hotels. Determine what the rates will be for individuals, families, and groups.

NOTES